For Debbie
enjoy
"Lucky"
7-16-9

Petted
by the Light

Petted
by the Light

The Most Profound and Complete
Feline Near-Death Experiences Ever

Patrick R. Tobin
and
Christine R. Doley

Illustrated by Christine R. Doley

A BIRCH LANE PRESS BOOK
Published by Carol Publishing Group

A BIRCH LANE PRESS BOOK
Published by Carol Publishing Group
Birch Lane Press is a registered trademark of
Carol Communications, Inc.
Editorial Offices: 600 Madison Avenue, New York, N.Y. 10022
Sales and Distribution Offices: 120 Enterprise Avenue,
Secaucus, N.J. 07094
In Canada: Canadian Manda Group, One Atlantic Avenue, Suite 105,
Toronto, Ontario M6K 3E7
Queries regarding rights and permissions should be addressed to Carol
Publishing Group, 600 Madison Avenue, New York, N.Y. 10022

Carol Publishing Books are available at special discounts for bulk
purchases, sales promotion, fund-raising, or educational purposes. Special
editions can be created to specifications. For details, contact: Special Sales
Department, Carol Publishing Group, 120 Enterprise Avenue, Secaucus, NJ 07094.

MANUFACTURED IN THE UNITED STATES OF AMERICA
10 9 8 7 6 5 4 3 2 1

Library of Congress Cataloging-in-Publication Data
Tobin Patrick, R.
    Petted by the light : the most profound and complete feline near-
death experiences ever / Patrick R. Tobin and Christine R. Doley.
        p. cm.
    "A Birch Lane Press book."
    ISBN 1-55972-314-9 (hc)
    1. Cats—Humor.   2. Near-death experiences—Humor.   I. Doley,
Christine R.   II. Title.
PN6231.C23T63   1995
818´.5402—dc20
                                                        95-19244
                                                            CIP

This book is dedicated to:

Brigitte Bardot
Doris Day
Debbie Reynolds
Betty White
and Bob Barker (before the controversy)
    for their tireless efforts on behalf of "all creatures
    great and small."

And whoever the guy is that wrote that.

Contents

Foreword

THE MOST DEFINITIVE BOOK on parazoology ever written, *Petted by the Light* offers more insights into animal near-death experiences than anything I've ever come across, including the masterwork *The Angel Wagged Its Tail* by Sister Connie. This is particularly impressive as I have studied hundreds of ANDES (Animal Near-Death Experience Survivors—*not* the after-dinner mints). From my years of study, I am convinced that animals know a heavenly light awaits. This is why they get that frozen stare at headlights. These poor creatures believe they are on their way to meet their maker. And I suppose they usually are, unless your brakes are really good.

Although much has been made recently of near-death experiences, all accounts have been from the human perspective. Such a genus-biased approach prevents us from gaining new information. For example, when someone has passed away, we sometimes say that he or she "croaked." Do frogs know something more about dying? And what about cats? If they have nine lives, do they have eight near-death experiences before kicking the litterbox? And with nine lives, what better research subjects for in-depth near-death study?

This book is important in that we need more believers in animal spirits. Many of today's problems, including our overcrowded pounds, the high rate of unwanted litters, and the hatred between dog and cat, cat and mouse, and mouse and gold-banded gibbon could be solved if creatures were more in touch with their spiritual side.

Petted by the Light is not just about the near-death experiences of eight different cats. It's about life, and it presents us with the higher meaning of all feline lives. Again and again their messages come across:

Purrs are heard.

We are all created as equals with the same access to kitty doors, sock drawers, and flower beds.

The best owner, the ultimate owner is God.

Live life to its fullest. Sit on sunny windowsills. Climb high trees. If you feel like it, quickly dart from one room to the next for no apparent reason. In fact, go ahead and knock over those garbage cans. Eat with gusto! Claw that new silk blouse your owner left on the floors! Go ahead and spray in your owner's house. Remember, it's your personal biosphere too!

In *Petted by the Light* we finally find the answer to the mystery that has baffled mankind for centuries: "What happens to Fluffy after she crawls into the engine on a cold winter night, and Daddy sets off for a beer run, thinking that the horrible, wailing, grinding noise from the hood was the transmission?" For those of us who have spent sleepless nights pondering such a question, peace of mind is at hand.

JOHN MCMUFFIN, V.D.,   D.M.V.

Acknowledgments

KUDOS TO THE ZOOLOGY DEPARTMENT of a prominent university on the West Coast. (Pending legal proceedings prohibit divulging the name, but it starts with a "B" and rhymes with "jerkly.") After all, we never would have written this book if it weren't for the committee rejecting our thesis proposal on Bovine Attention Deficit Disorder (B.A.D.D.). In a way, we owe them a small debt of thanks. That doesn't mean they should sleep any easier, however, because the suffering continues for millions of untreated, under-researched, overactive cattle.

We are truly grateful to the many people who *did* believe in us. They reassured us from day one, when we first heard of a black cat named lucky who had had a dramatic near-death experience. They also supported us during rough times. Like the time Joan Embrey threw us out of the San Diego Zoo for trying to talk to her precious ocelot, or when Christine came down with her unsightly mange. (By the way, Joan, your ocelot's a fake!) Thanks so much to our dear friends for their support. We should all be so committed.

Special thanks to Tim Didlake whose humor, suggestions, and Diet Cokes kept us going. And to all our family and friends for their love and support.

Pat and Tina

Lucky's Story:
Petted by the Light

My INSTINCTS TOLD ME that something was wrong. I had a feeling of foreboding, of impending doom. I believe that we all have a sixth sense, and many of my friends say mine is particularly keen. For example, when I dash up a Christmas tree, I sense its evergreen boughs wobbling long before it plummets to earth. I can perceive that the kitchen floor has been waxed just before I slide into the stove. And when I'm hanging on drapes, I can intuit the precise moment they'll give, and generally avert cat-astrophe. Yet for all my insight, I could never have imagined my experience on one very special day in 1988 when I had the honor to play in God's little acre, when I was personally petted by the light.

I've always thought a lot about death. Maybe my abiding interest was caused by something that happened to me when I was a mere mewing furball: I tried to race a closing garage door and lost. Pinned by a possessed automatic monster, I was unable to cry out for help. I struggled and gasped for breath. The next thing I knew, I was floating, released from the shackles of life. I looked down and saw a small kitten body sticking out from under the door. Then I floated straight through the garage door, and into the garage where I saw a little kitten head poking out. I recognized my own body, with a strange look of surprise on it. But this gruesome scene didn't affect me—in fact, I felt unusually happy. Then I remember flying to another place, a place I'd never seen but which felt utterly familiar. I met a beautiful Lion with a sparkling mane from which light seemed to emanate. He cradled me, and I felt completely calm and secure. I could have stayed with the Lion forever. But I heard a woman's voice say, "Why, she's still only a kitten, the poor dear." I awoke and found myself looking up at a rather large woman in an ill-fitting bathrobe. And that was how Josetta and I met.

Having survived the Genie accident, Josetta thought I was truly blessed and named me Lucky. Never mind that I am a black cat and most people groan at the name. She felt I was fortunate to have survived such an ordeal, and I eventually came to believe my name was fitting after all. Not for the same reason as Josetta, but because I had met the Lion, and had experienced his incredible love and compassion. I tried to explain this to Josetta, and to have an intelligent, comprehensive discussion with her about the afterlife, but she never understood what I was meowing about and only responded, "It's not time for dinner yet." I knew I would have to find answers elsewhere and just take comfort in the knowledge my experience gave me.

On the night of March 11, 1988, my keen intuitive perception made the hair on the back of my neck stand on end. I looked like a cheap Halloween card. Doom was in the air, so thick you could cut it with a knife! And a knife it was! For on March 12, 1988, I was spayed.

I had already had thirteen healthy offspring, and on the advice of my veterinarian and many animal-rights activists, Josetta decided it was the best thing for me.

Although I wouldn't have to hear any more stupid comments blaming my feisty mood on being in heat, I was as happy about it as one can be when they're about to slice you open like a cheap cut of beef. The night before my operation seemed endless. Thank God they gave me a knock-out drug so that I finally got the song out of my head.

I was suddenly awakened by a shooting pain in my tummy. I opened one eye and discovered I was on a cold steel operating table. I was freezing, thirsty, and in pain, but before I could muster up one little mew, I heard the vet say there was something wrong. This is not something you really want to hear when they're fiddling around with your plumbing, thank you very much!

All of a sudden I felt the life drain from me. And then there was this terrific pull, like someone was yanking me out from under the vibrating Barcalounger. I felt a pop and there I was, hovering inside the operating room. I started meowing at the vet, but he didn't seem to notice. "What is he doing to that odd-looking creature?" I thought.

Then I realized that little furball with the shaved stomach and the red collar was the reflection I normally see in the windows over sinks. That odd-looking creature was me! I was outside my own body! To tell you the truth, I was glad to be rid of its oppressive, unwieldy few pounds.

I saw three beautiful white kitties enter the room, hovering over the vet like hot air balloons. Their faces revealed the wisdom of the ages, so I knew they must have been really ancient. Even more prehistoric than the wheat germ in the back of Josetta's pantry. Without speaking, they told me that they were my guardian cats, and they were going to guide me home. "Back to the trailer park?" I thought. As if he could read my mind, one of the cats replied, "No, you're going to the big cat house in the sky."

I thought, "I can't be dying yet. I still have so much I want to accomplish." I was so close to figuring out how to open the lid to the fish tank. I wanted one more chance to pounce on something, anything. And I still hadn't finished that Concerto in G Minor, Opus 31.

My heavenly guardians seemed so benevolent and loving that what I'd left undone in my life didn't seem to matter. Then it dawned on me, "Wait a minute, I've smelled these cats somewhere before." I had known them even before I was born. They had been my choicest friends before I came to earth (well, to be more honest, they'd been my only friends, although I vaguely remembered a blind Siamese named Yogi who was always talking to his tail). I was filled with rapture as we reunited in levitation.

Then there was a loud sucking sound like that dreadful, wailing Mr. Eureka who drags Josetta all over the trailer. I felt myself being pulled up into a big black tunnel. We moved quickly through the darkness, the air rushing faster and faster. In all my life I've never understood why dogs get such a thrill from hanging their sloppy fat heads out of car windows. (Not to mention the fact that dogs are generally morons!) But now I felt like a moron and loved every second. Zipping through the blackness, I felt my whiskers flapping in the breeze. And it felt great, like I was going to face my destiny or slam into something.

There was a tiny speck of light at the end of the tunnel. The light came closer and closer and it had an amazing brilliance. Fearing the worst, I screamed, "TRAIN!" But my great wise elders just laughed. Soon the light was all around me, emanating from this incredible, loving spirit. Its illumination soaked me in a warm glow of love, sort of like a flea-bath but without the trauma. All my earthly burdens seemed to vanish. I'd never again worry that maybe I did look silly sleeping with my tongue hanging halfway out of my mouth. No more anxiety about whether I'd forgotten to kick some

"Its illumination soaked me in a warm glow of love, sort of like a flea bath but without the trauma."

litter over my business. Never again would I have to wonder if I ate some bad grass. The spirit felt so unconditionally loving, I knew I had finally found cat's best friend. I felt petted by the light.

Before I knew it, I was with my guardians again, flying over a huge park with piles of autumn leaves. I wanted to go down and play, but my mind was racing with question after question. Like, Are there fleas? No. Vaccinations? No. Children with water pistols? No. Had these terrors been eliminated, like my years of suffering for being a black cat? Yes. More questions followed, more yeses and nos. As soon as I thought of a question, it was answered. How do I see so well at night? What's really in kibble? Why do whales beach themselves? Instantaneously I comprehended volumes of knowledge. (Although I still never got a clear response about how the electoral college works.)

We passed through a pretty little town with many different stores: Cat's Meow, Purrfect Toys, Møuse, Lame Birds Я Us. At the Squeaky Toy Emporium each small toy squeaked heavenly praises, magnificent sounds that were indescribable. I was dying to go in and get my paws on a purple rubber mouse so I could squeak out Handel's *Messiah*.

I could've listened forever to the rapturous squeaks, but suddenly I heard the familiar voice of my vet. "I think she's gonna make it," I heard him say. I also thought I heard him mention something about malpractice insurance and his ass, but I honestly don't remember.

Then one of my guardian cats turned to me and said, "Lucky, you need to go back to earth." I didn't want to leave. I couldn't tear myself away from this place, which I knew was my rightful home. My guardian cat said, "Don't worry. You'll be back. But for now, your mission is not yet complete." And then I was floating through the tunnel again, right back into the operating room. My friends, the guardian cats, were there with me and they waited as I hovered over my body. It was all I could do to look at myself. I knew that I couldn't think about it or I wouldn't go through with it, so I popped back into my body. My friends nodded in approval and gave me a big thumbs-up (as best they could considering their lack of opposable digits).

That was two years ago. There isn't a day that goes by that I don't think about my near-death experience. And though I can't remember exactly what my mission is, I think it has something to do with spreading the message of love and acceptance. That, or maybe I should sleep more.

Josetta still doesn't know that she almost lost her little Lucky, which is fine by me. I know you want to know which vet I went to, so you can verify my story.

It's just, I don't want anyone to get hurt, especially Josetta. I know it happened, and that's all that matters.

Having died twice, and though I don't know whether it's true, I find some comfort in the rumor that cats have nine lives.

Bruno's Story:
Spritzed by the Light

I'M SICK OF HEARING all this crap about, "What's dog spelled backwards?" I've met the Big Guy and He ain't no Rin Tin Tin. Take it from me, he's one cool cat. Or "Tac." Get it, ya' stupid canine-lovers?

By the way, I don't know why you don't just do a whole book about me. If Marilu Henner can write her autobiography, who's to say my story's not as interesting, know what I mean?

I've spent my whole damn life in Phoenix and had over a dozen owners. Most of 'em were pretty godawful and didn't last very long. There was this elementary school teacher who started me on some special diet that was supposed to make me stop marking. Stuff tasted worse than the box it came in so I decided to show her, and I took a piss on the throw rug in the kitchen. Broad couldn't take me to the pound fast enough. Which reminds me of this other owner, a girl named Lisbeth who lived in a sorority house at ASU. I did my usual number on the sis to make her take me. You know, a little meowin', a little purrin', pretendin' I had nothin' better to do than rub against her hand. I never ate so good in all my life, 'cause there was always lots of leftovers. Thank God there was more anorexics than bulimics in that sorority house.

At any rate, would you believe that every single one of my owners called me Kitty Kitty?! About as original as a dog humping a human leg. The only name I'll answer to is Bruno, but I've yet to hear one of you human creeps call me that. Anyway, I have a pretty good thing going at the moment. My owner's a retired nurse named Edith and she lives out in a suburb of Phoenix called Sun City, which they should rename Geriatricsville, you know, with all those old folks zippin' around in golf carts like they was ten again.

The first time I almost died was when I got in a tangle with a surly raccoon who'd come down from the mountains. How was I to know he was a raccoon? I'm a city cat! I mean, all I said was "What the hell kinda cat are you, tubby?" You'd think the schmuck was royalty or something the way he reacted, I mean, he did *not* take it well. All he had to say was "I'm a friggin' raccoon," and I woulda left him alone. You don't wanna know what happened next. Let's just say my owner had a hard time finding the rest of my friggin' tail.

But that's pablum compared to the other time I really thought I'd be buying the farm, you know, pushing up daisies, cashing in my chips, shuffling-off-this-mortal-coil crap. It was just after I'd started living with Edith and she was having one of her bridge parties. I managed to sneak a piece of fried chicken off the counter, and I'd almost finished it when a bone stuck in my throat. It wasn't a very big one, so I start coughing, trying to get the damn thing up.

Well, I'm starting to make such a racket that Edith comes into the kitchen. Edith, bless her stupid little heart, thinks I've got a furball and she starts running around for the Petromalt until she and the old broads get distracted 'cause *Murder She Wrote* is starting. I was seeing stars and then everything went dark. Well, toots, I thinks to Edith, this is it. Sayonara, sister.

Then it was like I was pulled through a long tunnel. At the end there was a real bright light. I thought I was gonna go blind. I shot out the end of the tunnel like a bat out of hell and dropped right into the middle of a big desert.

I'm in the friggin' Sahara, I thought to myself. This dying thing's a bunch of crap, which was a pretty funny thing to say, considering the sand wasn't sand at all. "Whoa," I meowed out loud, "this is Tidy Cat Litter!" A whole desert filled with Tidy Cat Litter! That's when I knew this was heaven or the biggest friggin' cat box I'd ever see.

Then I noticed a loud sound comin' from what looked like a city. As soon as I heard it, I couldn't stop walking around in circles, meowing and drooling. Would you believe the buildings were actually giant crystal can openers going twenty-four hours a day?!

There was lotsa cats, all kinds of breeds and mixes. They were singing and dancing, like one big love-in. Hippies! Then I saw this huge field of catnip. So that's what it was; everybody was high. And the stuff was everywhere. You could roll in it and it wouldn't get smooshed. And you never got a hangover from the stuff. Not that I would know. I mean, I may have had it once or twice, but I never inhaled.

One of the cats shows me this big window. I look through it and I see some big blue ball spinning real slow with all these lights coming up from it. This cat tells me the lights are prayers coming up from the earth. Then he tells me each beam of light is heard and answered. And sure as spit, all these angels are flying around like a buncha silly schoolgirls, answering prayers. Some of the lights are stronger than others, 'cause some animals pray harder. One pretty bright light's coming from a mamma cat who wants her poor sick kitten to be all right. Another big beam is coming from this swan who can't find his mate. But the brightest of them all turns out to be coming from a dachshund in Cleveland. He's praying that this juicy steak will fall off the kitchen counter. Sure enough, an angel takes off for Ohio. The steak falls off the counter. Answered prayer. Then the owner comes in and smacks the hell out of the little wiener. Guess you gotta watch what you pray for.

I explore the city some more, and I see a group of cats batting around some clouds. That's right, clouds. Like the stuff you pull out of cheap furniture. These cats are playing some kind of volleyball with the clouds and they ask me to come join them. I usually don't go in for team sports, but it wasn't like Julie from *The Love Boat* is mapping out my eternity and I've got a million things to do. So I starts playin' with them.

Well, I was doin' fine until one of my claws sticks in the clouds. The more I pull, the more tangled I get. Before I know it, all the cats are laughing at me. "Just

"The more I pull, the more tangled I get."

you wait, you bunch of pusses!" I yell at them but I didn't really mean it. It's weird, up there in heaven, and I don't know why, but I was starting to feel nicer. And it felt nice to feel nicer.

So anyway, I'm still trying to untangle myself and I don't notice the cloud's getting higher. Before I knew it I was way above the city and the crystal can openers. Well, I decide I'm not gonna get all worked up 'cause I'm not in any danger, I mean I'm in heaven, right? It's not like I'm gonna die again.

Well, you're not gonna believe what happened next. I'm on this cloud, minding my own beeswax, when I sees God come racing across the sky with a squirt bottle in his hand. How friggin' typical, I thinks to myself. Everyone was playing and I'm gonna get stuck holding the ball. But God didn't look angry or nothin', not like that couple did when I took a test-claw on their new Ikea futon. God just started squirting me, laughing to Himself.

Well, I got untangled real good and fast and I jumped off the cloud, the water just missing me. And I'm fallin' and fallin' for what seems like forever. Except when I finally land on the ground this time I don't land on my feet, I land on my back! I keep my eyes closed, 'cause I'm thinking they're gonna have to scrape me up with a spatula. But when I opened my eyes, all I saw was Edith and her friends. I guess one of the old broads had just taken a first aid class at the rec center, so she'd given me a mini-Heimlich and got the chicken bone out.

You're probably thinking I've just made this whole thing up, and I'd agree with you if it wasn't for what happened next, and you can ask Edith if you want. But I swear to God (and I can do that, 'cause I've met Him) it was actually raining outside. "Raining in Phoenix?" you ask. All the old broads were saying that, too. And then I figured it out. God was just finishin' off his squirt bottle.

Lucky:
Bud Light

THE DAYS AFTER MY second near-death experience were carefree and filled with discovering anew the wonders of life. It was like being a kitten again. Colors and sounds, smells and shapes, all competed for my attention. Josetta's trailer became my oyster. I'd scour every inch of our home as if I were an explorer. An unmade bed became an island in the Pacific. Dust bunnies became my comrades and moths my mortal enemies. Empty Snickers wrappers were an obstacle course through the jungle of the kitchen.

I think I was starting to get on Josetta's nerves because one day she yelled at me, when all I was doing was playing with the clothes that she was folding. They were all so warm and toasty. How could I resist? And anyway, I was in the middle of exercising my creativity, battling a giant monster trying to suffocate me.

Okay, they were her panties. But that's no reason for her to yell those things at me. I know when I'm not wanted, so I decided to find somewhere to lie low. A trailer isn't exactly filled with places to hide, but I discovered a little cave where I was sure Josetta wouldn't find me. It was warm and toasty just like the clothes. I curled up and decided I'd take a little nap while my unimaginative owner cooled off.

Before I knew it I felt something cold and wet jump on top of me. I panicked! Maybe Josetta's panties really were trying to kill me. She's always saying they're killing her. I didn't have any time to fight back because the front of the cave closed and everything went pitch black. I struggled to find a way out, but suddenly the cave started turning upside down. I was thrown all over, tumbling with the wet creature. It became very hot in the cave and I thought maybe I'd had the misfortune of being in a volcano that was about to erupt.

I remember spinning upside down and hitting my head over and over. I don't know if I lost consciousness, but eventually the swirling turned into a dark whirlpool and I was drawn into it. I wasn't disoriented. Obviously I was dying again, and sure enough, my guardian cats were escorting me through the tunnel of light. I asked one of them if Josetta was going to die from the volcano too. He said, "Yeah, she's going to be fluffed and folded to death, Snuggles."

After we all had a good laugh, we were in the heavenly city again. Since I was last there, things hadn't changed much except they'd opened a new WalMart. One of my guardian cats asked if I wanted to visit the garden of delights, and since I didn't have any immediate plans I joined her. The garden was like nothing I'd ever seen in all my life. The plants and flowers and fruits were so colorful and beautiful that they seemed to pulse with life itself. I'd thought I'd seen the ultimate in the plastic fruit bowl and the artificial geraniums Josetta has on her coffee table, but now I knew I was seeing perfection.

I noticed a little brook that ran through the garden, and beside it was a strange little flower that stood out from the rest. It was singing a magnificent song of praise. I stood transfixed watching the bud gently sway in the breeze. Its lovely song beckoned, and I approached it with reverence. Then I bit it.

Before I really even got a taste of it, I felt myself

become the flower! I became the petals, and we were one together. I was the heavenly aroma! I was both the-singer and the song! I felt incredible; a wonderful part of a harmonious loving world. In this glorious floral communion, I realized, flowers have feelings, too. And you know, I haven't eaten another flower since.

I went to the far end of the garden.

"I felt myself become the flower."

There was a large building made entirely out of brilliant glass. I knew it wasn't someone's home, because there weren't any plastic deer on the front lawn. A cat waved me over and volunteered to take me on a tour if I liked.

Once inside, I nearly went crazy with joy. There were many cats who were busy clawing various pieces of furniture. My guide told me that in heaven cats get to fulfill their innate purpose of shredding sofas and chairs and rugs and drapes, which is one of the reasons God created cats in the first place. My guide asked me if I'd like to work there, too, but just as I was about to say yes my guardian cats showed up looking a little embarrassed. They said that they'd made a mistake and that Jesus had just told them that it wasn't my time yet. They'd been a little hasty after the dryer incident, because apparently Josetta got me out of there real quick and revived me.

Oh, well. At least the guardian cats and I all had a nice visit together. And wasn't I lucky to have a third chance to see heaven?

Cordelia's Story:
Lite Light

CAN YOU BELIEVE THIS portrait of me? I'm so fat I look like one of those Macy's Thanksgiving Day Parade balloons. No, I take that back. I look even bigger and scarier than a ten-story helium-filled Wonder Dog. The picture was drawn right before I almost died. (I'm not going to use pleasant euphemisms like *passed away* or *went to*

sleep because my friend, Princess, says I should embrace the truth and not pad it—which she says is actually a verbal metaphor for my weight problem, you know, padding myself from the truth of life.) It goes without saying that I was in complete denial. Totally out of touch with my inner kitten. Of course, I had to nearly join the *choir invisible* to learn this. Oh God, I'm using euphemisms again. It's not easy confronting the truth about my weight problem and, in general, about my entire life.

But I'm not bitter. I've even forgiven Jonathan, my owners' only child. You see, Jonathan thought he was going to make it into the *Guinness Book of World Records* by having the fattest cat in history. The little demon—whoops, I mean, Jonathan—only had twenty pounds to go. Oh, forget it, he is a little demon. Sorry. It's just that I have a long way to go, and Princess says it's okay to still feel the anger. So, I'm going to take a moment and give myself a mental *Attagirl*, because I've come very far, and every time I slip I get back up on the scratching post.

Jonathan's parents, Audrey and Maxwell, are both professors at Mount Holyoke. Of course, where else would two over-educated ex-hippie pseudo-intellectuals with overpriced, status-conscious bourgeois taste make a living, their only responsibility being to occasionally publish some lame-ass article about "Past-Imperfect Conjugation and the Post-modern Novel" and attend Chaucer conventions in Iceland? At any rate, they both encouraged Jonathan's abuse of me in the name of learning—it was like I was just another science experiment. Plus, they thought a Guinness Record might give him some much needed self-esteem. (Jonathan needed more self-esteem like the world needs more buddy-cop movies.)

Always happy to help foster young minds, I put up with it. Okay, so he wasn't exactly holding a gun to my head to make me eat. But you just try to ignore five servings of Tender Vittles a day. And Vienna sausages, too. Just thinking about them makes me purr. I mean, have you ever tried them with some nice spring nightingales? Only now do I clearly see how we were all contributing to put the "dys" in our barely functioning family.

Can you blame me for deciding to run away? I think not. Trouble was, I hadn't planned on being too robust for the pet door. You see, I hadn't gone outside in quite a while, so when I found myself stuck I was caught off-guard. Ever in denial, I kept pushing myself through the little door, chanting, "I can fit, I can fit," which naturally just made it worse. Then, just like a bad case of the clap, Jonathan showed up. From outside, he started tugging on my front paws until I became so wedged in the door that I couldn't breathe anymore. Jonathan, ever-observant scientist that he is, somehow hadn't noticed that I'd stopped breathing and was going limp and lifeless in his hands.

At least I didn't feel any pain, just the comforting sensation of losing consciousness. And then I saw the light. Words cannot express the beauty, the absolute incredible brilliance of this light. I was drawn toward the light and felt a happiness I've never known. The light didn't care that I was big as a house.

Somehow, before I knew it, I was on a great wide beach. I knew it was a beach because I'd seen most of Martha's Vineyard from a cat carrier one summer, but here the ocean was whitish. I know what they say about curiosity and the cat, but I was dead already so I went to the shore to investigate. The water was actually pure Grade A cream. A wave crashed against the shore and brought a new supply to me. I figured, what the heck, Jonathan couldn't get me in the record books now, so I lapped it up to my heart's content.

After a few minutes, well, okay, about an hour and a half, I decided to investigate the rest of the beach. I walked along the shore and saw a little knoll that was covered with window ledges, perfectly positioned to receive sunlight all the time! I jumped up on one of them and curled up in the dreamy heat. I was in cat heaven! I must have slept there for awhile, because

"So much cream, so little time. Wait a minute. I have all the time in the world."

when I woke up every part of my body was toasty warm. And you know, my tongue was dry as sandpaper. Okay, so it's always like that. But my only thought was another trip to the beach.

The sea was calm. I thought, so much cream, so little time. Wait a minute. I have all the time in the world. As I bent to drink, I saw my reflection. Each lap of my tongue created beautiful ripples that moved out to the horizon. My reflection shimmered. And then a strange thing happened. It was suddenly like I was with Audrey and Maxwell watching some Nova special about kittens. The images were three dimensional. Then I realized I was about to see a review of my life.

As it progressed, I not only reexperienced my own emotions but everyone else's feelings, too (which can be a little disconcerting given the psychological profile of our family). I saw myself as just a kitten at the Pawsitively Purrfect Pet Shop in downtown Westchester. I could see the enthusiasm of the shopkeeper. He seemed to think we would sell quickly. After all, it was almost Christmas. This became true for my brothers and sisters. I languished for weeks, then months. It became apparent that I wasn't going anywhere, even at a reduced price. I reexperienced the shame, the humiliation. Again I overheard the words that were to haunt me from that day forward: *runt of the litter*. How was I to know that

I didn't have all the genetic tools to become a champion Persian?

I watched Easter decorations go up, and that little kitten was still at Pawsitively Purrfect. The owner dropped my price to $39.99. I was two dollars less than the Dutch bunnies! But sadly, while they disappeared in droves, I remained. Then I saw Audrey and Maxwell. My shame turned into abject horror as I knew they were looking for a pet for Jonathan. I heard them tell the shopkeeper that Jonathan needed to learn responsibility and he could best learn that by taking care of a pet. Oh, why didn't they choose the aquarium? Jonathan thought my features were "weird" and that someone had "squished in my face." Audrey and Maxwell found his rudeness "cute" and after picking out a catbox, two dishes, a collar, a scratching post, and a brush, we were on our way home in their late model Volvo.

I wanted to stop the review. This was becoming too painful. I think I'd almost have rather been declawed than continue watching my life. But I knew in my heart I had to watch.

The review sped up, yet I could comprehend everything perfectly. I saw how my actions could affect others, like a ripple in a pool of cream. I saw how one little clawing of the couch could set Audrey off. And how in turn, she would snap at Maxwell, who then wouldn't play with Jonathan, who would finally take it out on me. And again, the emotions I felt watching these scenes were intensely real. For example, I actually became dizzy as I watched myself spin on the turntable.

Visions continued to speed before my eyes. I saw Jonathan playing kitty paratrooper with me. I saw my food bowl overflowing with mouth-watering cat chow. I saw Jonathan "verifying" that cats land on their feet nine out of ten drops. I saw Vienna sausages, chanting "Eat us, Cordelia. Eat us, Cordelia." I saw our little kitty submarine commando "game" in the bathtub. Dancing bowls of cat chow. Kitty crash test dummy. More chow. Sausages. Naps. Chow. Sausages. Naps. Jonathan, Jonathan, Jonathan!!!

As I fell to the sand and cried, it suddenly became clear to me. No one was forcing me to eat. I could've stopped when I was full, but something inside me hadn't cared that none of the tomcats found me worth even a second growl. I saw my justifications, telling myself those brutes were coarse and vulgar and common, and I didn't want their attentions anyway. But I'd finally hit upon the truth. The problem with my whole life was low self-esteem. From my first thoughts of being only a runt and unlovable, through all of Jonathan's tortures, I found comfort in my feeding bowl. As soon as I realized this I saw my last moments when Jonathan was pulling me through the pet door. And then the review ended.

I looked up and saw a giant bed beckoning me from off in the distance. I didn't find the sight of a giant bed out in the middle of nowhere unusual. I simply wondered if I could jump up on it. "But what if I break it?" Then I remembered something that gave me courage: I couldn't be as fat as I looked in the review of my life, because the camera adds ten pounds!

The bed felt like it went on forever and right in front of me was the biggest Sunday newspaper I've ever seen. I played with the paper for awhile, scattering it all over the bed, hiding under the comics section, sliding on the coupon pages. I was having the time of my life—I mean, death.

I felt something stir on the bed and poked my head up out from under the sports section. I was surprised to see a pair of giant legs underneath the covers. I walked over and tentatively brushed up against them. They were very warm and I felt completely safe, so I curled up right next to them. I started purring and shut my eyes.

That's when I suddenly felt the owner of the legs sit up in bed. I opened my eyes and imagine my surprise when I saw the face of God peering down at me! He started petting me and calling me "nice pussycat" and I purred even louder. And then He picked me up and held me right up to His face and said, "Cordelia, it's not your time, kitty." Then He said something about the secret of the Universe, but I didn't hear the last part of what He was saying because He was putting me back down. That's when I felt a hard tug on my body. Well, God had put me back in the pet door and Audrey had found me, and Jonathan got grounded. I knew that it was only a matter of time before he would exact his revenge upon me, so I decided I still needed to escape. And from that day on, I only ate one packet of Tender Vittles a day and an occasional Vienna sausage. When I'd lost about five pounds I managed to fit through the pet door, so I waited until late that night before taking my leave.

They never found me. I made it to the next county, where a nice woman named Linda saw me in her backyard and started feeding me. Before long, she let me come inside at night and, well, we're just the best of friends now. Why, she even listens to me and seems to understand what I'm saying. Sometimes I sit on Linda's shoulder while she reads and scratches me under my chin. Linda thinks I'm pretty and she can spend hours just brushing me and fixing my collar. My self-esteem now? Fabulous. Oh, and one other thing. Linda has the greatest windowsill, which gets about seven hours of sun a day.

It may not be heaven, but it's sure close.

Lucky:
Flying, Then Crashing
and Burning in the Light

WHOEVER SAID BLACK CATS were unlucky? I have to be the most fortunate cat alive. I've already survived dryers, garage doors, and incompetent veterinarians. I mean, I know they say that cats have nine lives, but how many cats do you know who've had even one near-miss? Yet,

I've knocked three times on death's door. Granted, for me it's a revolving door. Obviously I lead a totally charmed life. If you still don't believe me, read on:

- Josetta rents *Sleepless in Seattle*. She then decides that instead of being an insomniac in Reseda, she'd rather lose sleep in the Pacific Northwest.
- Our bags, packed; our garage sale, a success; our car, stolen. We decide to fly.
- The weather forecast is bad, the pilot is drunk, there's a problem with the plane, and Josetta forgets my stress tablets.
- To calm me, a baggage handler slips me a Valium.
- The forecasted inclement weather clears. Captain Vince Vodka sobers up. The short in the electrical system is noted and repaired. The Valium kicks in. It looks like we're in for a pleasant flight after all. Then, an albatross flies into an engine. The engines gaggle on geese.
- We quickly lose speed and altitude. We crash and burn.

As you can see, if it were not for an unlikely chain of events, I would not have died for a fourth time. And the chances of being resuscitated for a fourth time are probably even more remote. But because of the Valium, I was so relaxed that the damage to my body was less than lethal. Why, even being in the belly of the plane as it rolled over and skidded on its back proved serendipitous.

Tom Doe's Story:
Helluva Light

I DON'T WANT YOU TO USE my real name, so just call me Tom Doe. And don't let anybody know where I live, okay? If too many people find out where I live it'll be a circus at home, and I want to spare my owner that— God knows I've caused her enough grief as it is. Look, it's not personal, it's just that I had a really bad experience on *Geraldo*. The producers promised that my face would be blocked out and it wasn't, so now I've got the tabloids chasing me and linking me to Socks and so on. You get the picture. I got to be careful.

I'm sure you're getting all kinds of heartwarming,

fuzzy little stories about heaven and such, but I'm here to tell you a different kind of story. Maybe there's angels. Maybe there's a bright light at the end of the tunnel. Maybe Chuck Heston meets you at the pearly gates. But that's not the way it went for me. My story's about a cat who thought he had the world in his paws, who thought he was invincible, who thought death was just some loser he could laugh at. My story's a warning, if you will.

I used to be the head of a gang that controlled most of the catnip in the Southside. We dabbled a little in tabby slavery, trafficking of mice, and ran a couple of cat houses in the red light district. Anything to turn a profit—we didn't care if we were ruining lives. I remember turning nice little kittens from good homes into deranged, surly junkies, and I'd laugh while I did it. Everybody was scared of me: the birds, the mice, other cats, even my owner, and that's the way I liked it. Nobody was gonna tell me what to do or when to do it.

My owner had no idea what was going on. She'd leave for work in the morning and let me outside. Boy, if she only knew what I did! As long as I wasn't gone for more than a couple of days at the most, she never worried. I'll bet there's a bunch of other owners out there who'd be surprised to find out what their little Mitts or Toonces is doing while they're gone.

I didn't need anyone, period. There was this one little manx I had a real thing for one time, but she didn't want anything to do with me. She wanted a stud with class and the papers to prove it, the kind of cat she could have a nice little litter with. That kind of stuff used to make me sick. I wasn't a patsy. I felt only greed and hatred.

There was this house down the street that had the best catnip in the city growing right in the backyard. The dope was just there for the picking. Trouble was, besides the catnip there was a big German shepherd named Chauncy in the backyard, a real killer with a reputation for tearing apart cats like they were rag dolls. Well, that didn't stop us, 'cause me and my boys had a system where we'd wait for Chauncy's owner to take him for a walk, and then we'd go raid the catnip. It drove that fleabag Chauncy crazy, 'cause he could smell us after we left, but we were long gone, and there was nothing the bastard could do about it.

Now my right-hand cat, I'll just call him Max, I mean Joe, had always been reliable, especially when things got dangerous. But I suppose he was getting ambitious and greedy, just like every other cat under the sun. One night we decided to go harvest some of the catnip 'cause we had a big order from a couple of rich Persians on the other side of the tracks. Joe and the boys staked out

Chauncy's yard and gave me the caterwaul when it was clear. When I heard Joe give the signal I went running under the fence right toward the patch of catnip. I remember thinking I wasn't hearing the gang behind me, but I just figured that would leave more for me. I was a greedy bastard.

Trouble was, the son of a bitch Joe double-crossed me. I set off the motion detector light in the backyard and everything lit up like a parking lot. First and last thing I saw was that mangy mutt coming straight for me. I didn't even have time to talk my way out of the situation; Chauncy just opened his jaws and chomped down on me like I was a Milk-bone or something.

But there wasn't any pain, just a real comfortable darkness like going to sleep. At first I didn't think I was even dead, like maybe that mongrel had missed me or something. Then I heard a Voice coming through the darkness. The Voice didn't sound too happy. It called out my name so I answered it, like a loser, and then the Voice asked me where I thought I was. Well, I didn't really know but I told the Voice that since there was a good chance I was dead I was probably on my way to heaven. The Voice told me to think again. Uh-oh, I thought to myself, I'd better think up something real quick. I tried to reason with the Voice, you know, charm my way past the bouncer, so to speak. But I wasn't getting anything by this joker, no siree.

The Voice told me to quit stalling and said it was going to ask me one question and if I could answer satisfactorily I might not have to go to hell. Well, I'm pretty quick on my feet, so I figured a test would be just the ticket. That is, until the Voice asked me the question: "Can you think of one unselfish act of love you've done on earth?" What?! I was totally caught off guard. I mean, I thought the Voice was going to ask me to solve a riddle or something. You know, like there's a goldfish hanging from the ceiling and a puddle of water, with the door locked from the inside.

At any rate, I figured this question was going to be a breeze 'cause, I mean, how hard could it be to think of one unselfish act of love? At least that's what I thought. But every time I tried to think of something good, it was like I could see a dozen selfish or mean things I'd done. And not only would I see how rotten I'd been, I'd see and feel it from everybody else's perspective. All the bad things I did played on like a movie I couldn't turn off: the cat fights, the hissing, the bullying, the grand theft auto.

The memories eventually stopped, and there was dead silence. The Voice said, "Nice try, but no dice."

Then it felt like I was dropping off the top of a sky-scraper down into a real dark hole. I figured I'd be a cat pancake when I landed, but instead I splashed into water like a big rock. On my back! So water got in my ears and up my nose, which is just about the worst thing that can happen to a cat.

I shook myself dry and I could feel my fur trying to stand on end even though it was wet, which wasn't a good sign. I wiped the water from my eyes and looked around me. It was awful dark, but being a cat, I could see I was in the middle of a large tub of water right up to my knees. And standing in front of me was the biggest rat I'd ever seen, I mean, he was probably as big as a human.

I figured I was in hell. I looked around, and sure enough there were hundreds and hundreds of tubs with giant rats giving cats baths! Those poor pusses were all howling like they were being killed or something. And the giant rats were just scrubbing away, getting soap in our eyes and ears and everything. But that's not the worst part. When they were done scrubbing us, they'd dry us off with a humongous blow dryer, which was about as loud as a plane taking off. Then the rats would stick us back in the tub and it would start all over again.

I tried to smooth-talk the rat who was giving me a bath, but all he kept saying was *bad kitty,* over and over

"I figured I was in hell."

and over. I can't remember how many baths I got (I lost count after a gazillion). When the rat turned away to get more soap, I hightailed it out of there. I found myself in a dark room that looked like a big warehouse with only a couple of expensive-looking couches and drapes that blew in the wind, even though there really wasn't any wind. And there were pricey mirrors just hanging in the middle of nowhere. If I wasn't on the run from the rat pack, I would've stopped to see who was shooting the music video. I ran to one end not knowing where I was going. Besides a 7-Eleven in the distance, the only thing I found was a long, dark hallway with several doors. I opened one door to find a group of cats being chased by flying nail clippers! The cats couldn't get away, and when a set of clippers caught up with a cat it would snap away until there was nothing left but little bloody nubs.

Behind another door was a different group of cats that was trying to jump up on some windowsills, but each time one got up, the windowsill would turn into a molten piece of metal. The cat would screech and fall back to the floor, but the floor, would turn into slushy, wet snow. So the cats had to jump back and forth, back and forth, never getting comfortable. I hid my face in horror.

But wait until you hear what was in the next room. There were these models who were walking up and down a catwalk—literally! That's right, the platform was made up of hundreds of cats all squished together, and they'd bawl like a bunch of babies every time those high heels would pound down on them. The models all had names like Cindy and Naomi and Claudia. It didn't look like they were even breaking a sweat—they were just getting started.

I turned and saw a giant rat just behind me. Luckily I managed to leap from the monster's clutches. I could hear him behind me, chasing me and yelling that I'd never get away. Several times I could even feel his hot breath on my fur.

I ran inside a new room and the door shut behind me. I found myself staring at a classroom full of kids. There was this old teacher in the front who smiled at me real sinister-like. Then she told all the kids that it looked like the kitty was ready for show-and-tell. And before I knew it, some little girl with the stickiest fingers in the world came and picked me up and dragged me to the front of the class. She showed me to all the other little brats, and they all oohed and ahhed over me. Well, that was bad enough, being pawed by that little girl and her friends, all of them pushing and shoving. I noticed that their little hands were getting gooier and gummier. That's when I saw that the little fiends were actually sticking their hands in jars of honey and jam. And they started petting my fur the wrong way. I cried for them to stop, but that only made them push and shove and stroke even more. And then they started singing "It's a Small World After All," out of tune!

The teacher kept saying, "There is no rush, you kids have all of eternity to play with Kitty." I tried to figure out where I'd heard the teacher before, and then it dawned on me. She was the owner of the Voice. The woman smiled and asked me how I liked hell. I told her she should have asked me that question instead of the one about unselfish acts. She shrugged and said that we were only getting started.

I couldn't imagine what would be next. Crazy grandmas with rocking chairs? Fleas the size of hawks? Endless reruns of *Lassie*? Then the woman picked me up and took me somewhere. I couldn't make out what was going on, but as we got closer it looked like a doctor standing over a cat on an operating table. I screamed in horror. I was being given a second chance, although in her opinion I didn't deserve one.

Well, I was the happiest cat in the whole world. I was so happy I was ready to kiss the woman on the cheek, but she didn't look too thrilled about it, so I just purred a little to show my gratitude. She said not to thank her but to thank God, and she kind of mocked Him by saying things like He always has to be giving creatures second chances and how it screws up everything for her. I asked her if she was the Devil. She said that she wasn't—that title belongs to the guy who designed the 1040 IRS form. She was Death. I shuddered, considering how close I'd come to kissing her on the cheek. I mean, I hear some humans say they've looked death in the face and laughed, but obviously they haven't got my perspective on the matter.

Anyway, Death put me back in my body, and right before she did it she said that she'd be keeping an eye on me. I told her I hoped we wouldn't meet again. Then I felt like I was Thanksgiving stuffing being shoved into a turkey's butt. I guess it was hard making my spirit fit back into my body, kind of like humans trying to fold a map back up right.

Boy did I ever hurt! I must have been in a million pieces from that old Chauncy. The vet was a whiz, though, and I heard him finally tell his assistant to go tell my owner that I'd make it. My owner was so happy that I kind of choked up. I mean, all I'd ever done was take advantage of her and everybody else and still she loved me. She took a couple weeks off work to nurse me back to health, and she even used up all her vacation days! What a true friend.

I should be going 'cause I don't want to be late for my volunteer work. I'm trying to find some homes for a couple of feral kittens. There's just one last thing I want to say to all cats. Take it from me. You want to live your life right, keep your whiskers clean, and stay out of trouble. And that's about all I got to say.

Lucky:
Gaslight

By the time Josetta and I had been out of the hospital for a few weeks, you could barely see the scars left from the airline accident if you squinted your eyes. We'd settled nicely in the rainy Evergreen State and things were getting better. Or at least I thought they were. I would come to learn that Josetta wasn't feeling as good as I'd thought.

First, Josetta was homesick and sick of the rain. Second, because her eyebrows had been permanently singed off in the crash, Josetta was in a lot of pain. I think she got hooked on Extra-Strength Tylenol with codeine. I figured she had to be drugged because she watched the Racquetball Channel for hours on end. We had managed to unpack all our belongings that made it through the crash, which amounted to one outfit and a spoon. The Red Cross had been very nice and given Josetta and me several new things. A lot of these belongings looked pretty much like the stuff we'd gotten rid of at our last garage sale. I was comforted by this, but I think Josetta was depressed. And things only got worse.

Some other medicine Josetta took made her bloated. Well, she said it was bloating, but if you ask me she was retaining more than just water.

One Monday evening, she'd just come home from another day pounding the pavement, and again she'd had no luck finding a job. Josetta threw her bag down and collapsed on the chair by the card table. Which then, unfortunately, collapsed on the floor. It was the last straw, not only for the chair, but also for Josetta. She began to sob unceasingly. I tried to rub against her legs to calm her down, but she actually kicked me away.

I don't hold it against her though, because I know it was just a reflex, and as soon as she did it she cried even harder. She came over and picked me up, crying and stroking me and apologizing all over herself. She sobbed, "Look what I've done, I can't do anything right. And I'm taking it out on my only friend. I don't deserve to live."

Then the tears stopped. She sniffled and tried to compose herself. Something clicked, and she seemed a changed woman. With resoluteness she grabbed a pad of paper, a pen, and a bottle of wine. She unscrewed the wine and filled her Jurassic Park mug to the top. She began to write with intense concentration. Then, unsatisfied, she'd scribble, crumple, and write some more, recomposing note after note.

Finally there was no paper left. Josetta looked at the cardboard backing and took a deep breath. She wrote something on it, kissed the top of my head, and put me on the front porch.

Outside I jumped up on the window ledge. I saw Josetta go into the kitchen and open the stove. She turned on the gas and sat down on the floor near the oven door. I was very curious about what she was doing, because I don't remember her putting any actual food in the oven. I felt certain the note would explain it all. If only I could get back in to read it. Then I remembered that Josetta always left the bathroom window open for the kitty litter to air out. Once inside I ran into the kitchen. It smelled awfully strange in there and Josetta had fallen asleep on the floor. This seemed quite unusual to me. I thought how ironic it was that she had been sleeping a lot in Seattle. I jumped up on the counter to read the note. It said, "There is no paper left. I am too upset to live anymore. Goodbye cruel world. P.S. Please contact my nephew Johnny, to take care of Lucky for me." And that was the last thing I remember before blacking out.

Guess where I found myself for the fifth time? It's a good thing there isn't a toll booth in that tunnel of light.

Well, we both survived, and I feel like a hero. If I hadn't been convulsing on the counter, the neighbors would never have seen through our curtainless windows and found Josetta and me in time to rescue us. I'm beginning to think Josetta doesn't lead a very charmed life.

Baby's Story:
Corralled by the Light

My name's Baby, and I live in Dallas, Texas, the center of the world. If you don't believe me, well, that's too bad, 'cause it obviously means you've had a severe injury to your head that's affected your ability to reason. And that's enough said about that.

Most folk don't know what a hairless Sphinx is so I have to explain right off that I'm not a damn chihuahua with a vitamin deficiency. If y'all think I'm butt ugly, well there's nothing I can do 'bout it, 'cept say I'm not the only creature in God's green earth that's got a face only a mamma could love. Why, just take a peek at those armadillos or possums or even Mr. Perot if you don't think I'm speaking the truth.

Besides, when some uppity cat stares at me like I was the Devil himself, I just tell him he can stare all he wants, that don't change the fact that I'm a true-blue, dyed-in-the-wool show cat. That's right, with the papers to prove it. And I've been to the CFA invitational. Twice!

I live in a condominium right near downtown Dallas. Gail and Rex don't have young 'uns 'cept for me. I sp'ose that's why they call me Baby. Now, you didn't hear it from me, but once I heard Gail tell Rex he was shooting blanks (and we're not talking 'bout guns) and she started cussing at him 'bout how he couldn't even do this one simple thing right. But that's a whole other matter, and I don't think I want to start gossiping. Like it says in the Good Book, don't go biting the hand that feeds you.

My dying incident's not as glamorous as most, I'm sure, but it's my own story. And I'm proud as peaches 'bout it. I guess it all starts with Miss Gail. You see, she was seeing a special doctor, a gentleman Rex called the "shrink" (though it seems there's nothing small 'bout this man, 'specially his bills). Not that she told Rex, but Dr. Shrink started Gail on some special medicine for her nerves, and every morning I'd see her pop one of these little green-and-yellow pills. The pills are Pro-Zach, which I sp'ose must please this gentleman Zachary, whoever he is.

Now, I'm not sure if those pills helped her calm down, 'cause it's hard to tell with someone who's packing down a fifth of bourbon every other day, but she seemed mighty pleased with them, or so she'd tell all her girlfriends. Let me tell you, every one of those women is a taco short of a combo plate. Why, I swear the whole bunch of them have lead in their shoes so they don't go floating away, that's how empty their heads are!

Anyway, there's nothing Miss Gail don't start than sooner or later Rex goes and does the same thing. 'Cept he's real secret 'bout it so she didn't have any idea he was Pro-Zach, too. But I'm jumping ahead a myself.

One morning Gail was sitting at her vanity trying to pull her chin up real tight (good luck, honey, is all I can say) and she noticed me on the bed and declared I looked a little skittish. Of course I was only stretching, but you know Miss Gail, she'd be telling that old tortoise in the fable to slow down if he'd been racing her before noon. So I just ignored her and tried to finish my nap in a little peace and quiet. Well, before I knew it, she'd gone and got one of my treats and stuck half a green-

and-yellow pill in the middle. She buys these little treats special at Neiman-Marcus and I can tell you honestly they are just 'bout the best thing you ever did taste, next to rotten Chinese food in the garbage can. I think I'd just 'bout eat anything if it was stuck in one of those little treats.

Well, after that Gail started giving me half a pill in a treat every morning, right after she'd take her own pill. At first I didn't feel or act any different, and she was terribly disappointed. So she upped the dose to a whole pill. Now, one day 'bout two weeks after getting those pills, they started affecting me something awful. I thought I was going crazy, I couldn't sleep anymore and I ran around like a chicken with its head cut off. Seemed anything would set me off in a bad mood, too. Rex must've noticed my outlook was changing, cause he started giving me one of his little green-and-yellow pills stuffed in a Neiman-Marcus treat. Now you gotta remember that these two rocket scientists aren't talking to each other (on account of something Rex said to his sixteen-year-old sister-in-law when he was a little tipsy) so they've got no idea their little Baby's popping two of them green-and-yellow pills.

Hoo wee! Those pills were making me sicker'n a dog (don't that phrase just make a whole world of sense?). And to top it off, the worse I got the more pills Gail and

Rex would give me. It got so bad that I would just run around the bedroom all day, like one of them fool greyhounds chasing that metal rabbit. One time Miss Gail tried to make me stop, and I nearly bit her hand off. And I'd just hiss at old Mister Rex so bad he'd declare that Gail must've put me up to acting like that.

Y'all can see I was on a one-way trip to disaster and the two of them were piloting the plane.

And sure enough, one morning I just didn't get up at all. I remember trying with all my strength, but I wasn't even able to open my eyes, let alone move a muscle in my body. Next thing I remember it started getting awful cold, like that fool Gail'd left the A.C. on full blast in the middle of winter, which she's done on more than one occasion, mind you. Well, the cold must've started affecting my thinking cause everything got real muddled and foggy, to the point where I wasn't even sure where I was (now I can say I know how Gail and Rex feel most of the time!). And then it seemed like a dream, and I was floating over myself. I distinctly remember thinking that I wasn't half as ugly as folk had led me to believe—why, I was even kinda cute, in a Jim Henson sort of way.

I didn't float very long before I was back in my body again. I finally got my eyes open, but my vision was very, very fuzzy. I could barely make out a figure at the end of the hallway who kept saying "Here, Baby . . . come here, Baby." I thought it was Gail with a treat, so I got myself up and jumped off the bed and nearly fell flat on my face! Why, I was walking just like a baby kitten and it was all I could do to keep my balance. I tried to walk to the person saying my name, but the hall was getting narrower and longer with each step I took. I figured it was just those green-and-yellow pills playing tricks on my eyes.

Well, I kept walking for what must've been an eternity, but the person calling my name didn't get any closer. Now I was certain Gail had had Rainer, her "flight attendant by day, decorator by night" friend, over to remodel, 'cause it would be just like that fool to make a hallway just like a Habitrail or something like that. Then I noticed that the end of the hall was awful bright, even brighter than the sun, 'cept you could look at this light as long as you liked.

I didn't know where in tarnation I was, but I swear on a stack of Bibles that ol' bright light was starting to make me feel better. And not only was I feeling like myself again, I was feeling better than I ever felt in my whole life! And my muscles were starting to work right. Why, I felt so good I started running toward the end of the hall. And did I ever run! I'm sure I was running at least a hundred miles an hour, the walls just racing by me, just like that time Rex took me for a ride in his new red sportscar, with that young woman he kept introducing to folks as his niece, but I don't think a person's sp'osed to kiss his niece like that.

Well, before I knew it I ran right out of that hall, flew through the air, and ended up in the arms of a woman!

And do you know who that woman was? It was none other than Miss Dorayne Flood, the owner of the little pet store where Gail and Rex bought me. I was overjoyed with happiness, cause she was just 'bout the only nice human I'd ever known, but I was a little confused too. Why, I hadn't thought 'bout Miss Dorayne in years, and last I heard she'd gone and bought the farm, if you know what I mean. She must've read my mind 'cause she told me "You heard right, Baby."

Miss Dorayne put me down, and that's when I noticed where I was. We were standing in the middle of that ol' pet store of hers! Why, there was even the same blue-and-green neon sign in the front window, NOAH'S ARK blinking on and off (Miss Dorayne wouldn'ta called it anything else, what with the last name of Flood).

I asked her why, if we were dead, we were back in Noah's Ark. She explained that after we die we get to set up house anywhere we want. Like some folk decide they want to live on an island in the Pacific. Others pick a shopping mall. Some even decide they want to sit around on clouds all day and play harps.

Miss Dorayne took me around the store and reintroduced me to some of my former shopmates who had already met their Maker. There was Ginger, that crotchety ol' parrot who nobody bought 'cause she swore like a truck driver. Ginger was quite pleasant and obviously somebody had told her to keep a lid on her lips, cause she didn't hardly cuss one bit. (Actually I was little surprised to see Ginger there, if you know what I mean, but I guess that's why only the good Lord can judge and not us, right?) I also saw those two talkative Tabby sisters, Ellie and Kate, and it turns out they'd ended up with some Air Force officer and his family who traveled all over the world.

Well, I figured we were gonna spend half of eternity just listening to the sisters when Miss Dorayne suddenly looked at her watch and said we had to hurry. I said a quick good-bye to everybody as she picked me up and we went outside the pet shop. We were met at the curb by an old Checker cab, and we piled inside. You're not gonna believe who was driving the cab. Why, it was none other than the Lord Jesus Christ Himself. And let me tell you this much, He sure don't look at all like that velvet painting Gail's aunt gave her two Christmases ago, the one that Rex gave to Goodwill the very

"You're not gonna believe who was driving the cab."

next day. Fact is, he looks a lot like Omar Sharif, 'cept way more handsome and without the funny accent or gambling problems.

Jesus tipped his cap to me and said a friendly howdy, but I was speechless. That didn't seem to bother Him one bit and He and Miss Dorayne seemed to be just the best of friends, so I decided to relax a little and say a proper hello. Jesus drove the cab down the street and started pointing out various houses. He showed me where Lady Godiva and Mr. Ed live, I guess the two of them get along like peas in a pod. And He showed me where Colonel Sanders has built a mighty fine home for chickens (I sp'ose it's his way of saying sorry). Oh, and I just went crazy over this one house on a lake, where Flipper and Johnny Weismuller live.

Jesus said that animals and humans get along real fine in heaven. Miss Dorayne nodded and said she'd been waiting for me to get to heaven 'cause I was the one animal she just couldn't do without. Well, that was definitely the sweetest thing anyone has ever said to me, 'specially since I look just like a bat with a hormone problem. Jesus must've known what I was thinking, 'cause He asked me if I'd ever seen a bat with a hormone problem. And I had to confess that I hadn't. So He said that I should stop worrying 'bout what I look like and concentrate on being the best me, 'cause that's the way He made me and it's nobody else's concern. And Miss Dorayne said a big "Amen!"

Before I knew it, Jesus had driven us right up to Gail and Rex's condo building. 'Cept nobody could see us. Jesus put the cab in park and let the engine idle. And He asked me if I wanted to stay with Him and Miss Dorayne, or go back and finish my business with Gail and Rex. I didn't know what that business was, but I think Mister Jesus wanted me to go back, 'cause the door opened by itself. So I got out of the cab. I thought I'd be just torn up, leaving the two of them, but as they both waved at me with the biggest smiles you ever did see I felt a peace 'bout the whole thing. And I watched as that ol' cab drove off and then rode up into the sky straight up to heaven.

Well, I wasn't sure what to do next, but I didn't have to stand there very long and think. Gail and Rex were rushing out of the front door holding my limp body in their arms. They both looked a frightful wreck, and Gail was really crying. As they brushed right by me I felt myself slip back into that old body of mine. Boy, it was like getting slapped in the face with a cold, wet sock, seemed like I weighed a ton and half.

They rushed me to the vet awful fast. Only other time I saw them move that quick was when their accountant called up and said they were gonna be visited by the IRS. Well, that vet just 'bout spayed and neutered the two of them when he found out what had been going on with the pills and such. He told them he wasn't even sure I'd make it. I knew I would, but still it was kind of fun to hear Gail and Rex worry a bit. After the vet emptied my stomach and got me all flushed out, I woke up and started to get better. And Gail and Rex were mighty relieved to hear that I was gonna make it after all.

'Bout a week later I finally went home, and they took real good care of me. And you know, there is such a difference in our home now. I guess my mission is to help Gail and Rex think 'bout something other than themselves. Not that my mission's over yet—and not that it's the easiest thing in the world. Not by any stretch of the imagination. I mean, they're still Gail and Rex, but they're getting there. And as long as I keep getting treats from Neiman-Marcus, I don't mind at all how long it's gonna take.

Lucky:
Snuffed by the Light

THERE WAS NOTHING TO LIKE about Josetta's nephew Johnny. Let me put it in perspective. After one week with him, I was wishing they hadn't saved me and Josetta from the gas. What's wrong with him? Where do I begin?

First, he never got me real catfood. Instead, he fed me the same generic junk he fed his dog Gus. Which brings me to the second thing. Gus. Stupid, flea-ridden, never had a bath, drooling, Gus. I could tell you things about Gus that would make your stomach turn—his halitosis, his flatulence, his predilection for mating with cheap pieces of furniture—but I don't think I need to go into detail.

Johnny didn't believe in providing me with a litter box, so I had to go outside. And Gus would leave these humongous droppings all over, so there was never anyplace I could call my own. Could Johnny ever clean up the yard? Could Gus learn to cover his turds? Is the Pope Jewish?

Johnny loved hunting. Since the only thing he kept clean in the house was his gun, I wasn't surprised. Except Johnny was lazy, too, so he never actually went hunting. He'd just shoot at beer bottles on a fence and occasionally read some magazine called *T&A* (for Traps and Ammo, I think). Sometimes Gus would snoop out a couple of squirrels and Johnny would take a shot at the poor little creatures.

One afternoon Johnny was home with a couple of friends, and they were watching a football game and drinking an awful lot of beer. During the halftime break, they took the empties and started shooting at them.

Well, I nearly went crazy with all the racket, and I tried to hide under the couch. Except that fink Gus started barking at me, so all the guys came inside to find out what was going on. When they saw Gus trying to scare me out from under the couch I heard Johnny say how much he disliked cats. And those pigs he calls friends all said they hated cats, too.

I don't know about you, but when a bunch of drunken idiots load every gun they have and start screaming "Let's get some wildcat," you don't hang around to argue with them. Gus, the little traitor, played right along and started chasing me through the woods behind Johnny's house. I swear I even heard a banjo playing.

I was absolutely terrified, but even in my horror I remember thinking how ironic my name was. And I started snickering. That's right. Snickering. Snickering like a fool.

My guardian cats later asked me what was so funny, but I couldn't stop laughing long enough to answer them. They told me to come to my senses, which only made me laugh harder, considering all of my senses were back on earth. I guess they read my mind. They offered to bring me back, but I said, "Don't bother, I know my way." And before I left, (for the sixth time), I told them I was dropping Lucky and changing my name to Jinx.

Fabio's Story:
Scrooged by the Light

Fɪʀsт ᴛʜɪɴɢ ɪ ᴡᴀɴᴛ ᴛᴏ sᴀʏ ɪs, everybody who still likes Garfield is a total loser. And you're a total loser to the infinity degree if you think your cat's just like him, 'cause we're not at all. I'm not just saying that 'cause some bogus pet shrink said I'm a troubled teenager. I mean, how would you feel if all us cats started saying, "Oh, I love Andy Capp, 'cause my owner's just like him"? Yeah, I'm sure you're gonna want to be compared to some drunk who sleeps around and who can't hold down a job.

You humans are so weird, I don't think us cats will ever be able to figure you out. I mean, it's common knowledge that we were worshiped in Egypt, right? All those Egyptians thought we had magical powers or something. Yeah, and I've got a bridge I'd like to sell you. I hear the dogs in Egypt tried to get in on the action, but they're not half as cool as cats. I mean, their smell alone is enough to make you sick, and they've always got their noses up someone's butt, which is totally gross. Can you imagine having a hieroglyphic picture of that on your tomb, so that's what future generations remember about you? I don't think so.

Like most humans, my owner Ted can be really stupid sometimes. Like, he bought this video that they were advertising on TV. *The Well-Behaved Cat* shows how you can train your cat to sit in your lap all the time and purr like a kitten. Why didn't he just go and give me a lobotomy if he wants a cat like that?

The video had this English chick who sounds like a dork and she had this cat in her lap who looked like he was stoned. And the English chick started petting the cat with this feather, and that was supposed to make him behave. For this, Ted paid forty bucks!

He's convinced I've got behavior problems, which is a bunch of BS. He's just being mean 'cause his girl-friends like me better than him. And I think he's mad 'cause I don't act like a stupid little kitten. He always expects me to sit by him. And he asks me why I don't purr that much anymore. I'll tell you why. It's 'cause I don't like him telling me what to do, and I especially don't like him cuddling with me. It's just not cool anymore.

For a couple of weeks he tried using the quill and "positive affirmation" method from the video, but he gave up on that pretty quick, especially after one of the scratches I gave him got infected.

I let him know I wasn't happy with the whole situation. Whenever I used my box I'd make sure to miss the cat litter. And one time Ted left his wool slacks on the floor, so I decided to make them shorts instead. And then another time I jumped out on the balcony rail and scared the living daylights out of him. Yeah, like I'd ever fall, Ted. Duh! I'm not the uncoordinated geek.

I'm not saying I don't like Ted. He's a pretty okay owner, and my situation is definitely not the worst one a cat could be in. I mean, who would want to be Socks, slinking around the Rose Garden trying to take a dump with about a hundred cameras following you? I try to stay out of trouble, but it's really hard sometimes. If Ted would just leave me alone everything would be great. Like, if he didn't keep spanking me every time I chewed on the lamp cords I probably would've stopped on my own. But Ted has to go sticking his nose in my business. So I'd spend all day sleeping, then the minute Ted got home I'd chew on the lamp cord, while he was changing out of his suit. And he'd come out of the bedroom and see me chewing the cord and then he'd yell and chase me all over.

I couldn't understand why it bugged him so much. I should've known there was probably some good reason, especially after I got a little shock one time and Ted saw me jump and he said, "There, you got what you deserved." But I figured he caused the shock somehow, just to be mean, so I didn't really think about it that much.

One afternoon I'd just finished a nap and I was looking for a little fun. I'd already worked over the front of one of Ted's speakers with my claws, and his chair was already covered with hair, so I decided to chomp a little on my favorite piece of plastic. Ted wasn't even home, so it wasn't like I was being a bad cat on purpose. I'd worked away one section pretty good, so I thought that I'd go ahead and finish the job.

I bit through the lamp cord with all my strength, until I tasted something metal. Before I knew what was happening I saw a white flash, and then it felt like someone had picked me up and thrown me toward the ceiling. I seriously thought Ted had come home and found me, except I was stuck on the ceiling and didn't fall back down. When I opened my eyes, I was looking straight down toward the floor. The only thing I could see was my body lying near the lamp. It took me a second to figure out the body was mine and that it was dead! Whoa! Was Ted gonna be P.O.'d or what? I could just hear him saying, "I told you so!" I'd bitten the lamp cord in two.

I tried to creep back down the wall to my body, you know, thinking I could just slip back in and pretend everything was cool again. But as soon as I'd get near my body, I was thrown back up to the ceiling. About the third time this happened I realized someone had come in, and it wasn't Ted. Standing near the door was the English chick from the video, holding a feather in her hand! Her lips were kind of pursed real tight. She didn't say a word, but I suddenly understood we could communicate without speaking. I tried to slink down the wall again.

"And where do you think you're going, Mr. Fabio?"

"I was just going back into my body, that's all," I explained. "Don't mind me . . ."

She shook her head and walked over to my body and gave it a little poke with the feather. "It doesn't appear that's very likely, now does it?"

I had to agree that I was dead, so it wasn't very likely

at all. The English chick reached up to the ceiling and gently pulled me down. I tried to get away from her, but her grip was very tight.

"There, there, let's be a good kitty." She held me so tight I could hardly move.

Worse, she carried me on my back like a little baby. "Who are you?" I asked.

"I'm Prudence, the ghost of owners past," she told me. "And I've come to teach you a lesson."

"Are you going to use the feather?"

She just snorted and shook her head. "I think I'll have to use something a little more effective on the likes of you, Mr. Fabio."

Before I knew it, we were walking through the wall and we ended up in an animal shelter. Something about the shelter was familiar to me, but I couldn't put my paw on what it was.

"I've been here before, haven't I?"

"You are correct. This, Mr. Fabio, is the shelter where you were brought after you were born." And she walked up to the cat section where there was a cage full of kittens playing with an old piece of string.

"Hey, that's my litter!" I said. Prudence put me down, and I ran up to the window of the cage. "There's my brother Kitty and my sister Kitty, and there's my younger brother Kitty." I was really happy to see them again. It was weird though, seeing myself running around and playing with the others.

I saw Ted coming into the cat section and he was looking at each cat really carefully, like he was buying a diamond or something. Just like Ted, can't ever make up his mind about anything. I saw him bend down to my cage and tap the side of the glass with his fingers. I almost wanted to pounce on Ted's finger myself, but Prudence held me back. None of my brothers or sisters noticed Ted's fingers except me. I remember thinking Ted was the coolest human I ever met, it was like he could do no wrong. Boy, how things had changed.

"You had good times with Mr. Ted, didn't you?" Prudence asked.

I nodded as I watched Ted point me out to one of the shelter employees, who then handed me to him. I was really small and I purred like crazy. Ted told the employee he couldn't wait to adopt me.

Then there were other scenes from my kittenhood to view: the times Ted would take a shoelace and play with me for hours, and how I used to chase his legs underneath the covers. I also saw how I used to sleep next to Ted because I wanted to. The thing that amazed me was how much I used to like being with him. And he seemed to like being with me, even when I had a little trouble with the whole litter box concept. Man, if

I had to pick up someone's poops I would not be as calm as Ted.

Prudence took me back to the apartment where my dead body was. "I think you've seen enough of your past. Now I leave you for the ghost of owners present. Try to remember, Mr. Fabio, that a well-mannered cat is a happy cat." And with that she disappeared, leaving me to stare at myself lying on the ground.

It wasn't long before the ghost of owners present showed up. He was this really old guy with white hair who was wearing a golf shirt and white pants. "Are you . . ." he pulled out a piece of notepaper in his pocket and read, ". . . Fabio?"

"Yes," I said, "are you the ghost of owners present?"

He seemed confused until he looked at the notepaper again. "Right," he finally mumbled, "but you can call me Marlon." He held out his hand, and I shook it with my paw. "Marlon Perkins the name, animals are my game."

Marlon tried walking through the wall like Prudence did, but he ended up hitting his head twice, so we used the door instead. Marlon and I walked toward downtown. "Flavia . . ."

I had to interrupt him and correct my name.

"Right, anyway, Floggio, our adventure starts in the

natural environment of the adult *homo sapien*." I saw Ted having lunch with some babe at an outdoor café.

"Hey, Marlon, there's my owner, Ted."

Marlon took off his reading glasses and squinted. "Hmm, yes, a full-grown adult male. We will call him Ted. His approximate age is believed to be about thirty. You can tell by his receding hairline."

I stopped listening to Marlon and watched Ted in action. I take back the part about the chick being a babe. She was a total babe and a half. He was sure trying to impress her, and I don't blame him.

I saw Ted try to touch the chick's hand at one point, and she pulled it back almost like Ted's hand burned her or something. Geez, she wasn't gonna cut him any slack. Every time he talked she'd look around like she was bored. She was even kind of flirting with the waiter, but Ted didn't seem to notice. Marlon did, though.

"The female is selective. She makes herself approachable to the male whose genes she wishes for her offspring. Watch as she avoids eye contact with the male who is seated. In this way she sends him the message that she is not interested in bearing his offspring."

Though the babe was totally ignoring Ted, he was trying to keep the conversation going. He did his impression of me, which I personally find totally funny, but she didn't even look at him. Then as he told her the story about how I used to chase his legs under the covers, he accidentally knocked over her glass of iced tea. It all spilled into her lap.

"There we go with the first stage of the mating ritual," Marlon said. "Marking the female to make claim that she is his and his alone is classic behavior in a social setting. Obviously the male is unsure of his adequacy in this situation."

I shook my head in humiliation. All I could say was thank God no one saw me there. The woman disappeared into the bathroom in a real snit, and there was poor Ted, trying to ignore everyone who was looking at him like he was a king-size deluxe dorkorama.

"Looks like the female human has rejected the male's advances. She definitely looks hostile," Marlon rambled on. And on. And on.

After I got over the humiliation, I felt really really sorry for Ted. And I was about to say that to Marlon when I realized he was gone. The old geezer just disappeared. That's when I saw Prudence waiting at a bus stop. She was reading the *Times* and glanced up at me.

"Where's Marlon?" I asked.

"Your guess is as good as mine," she said as she stood up and opened up her umbrella. "Let's fly."

"You can't be the ghost of owners future, can you?"

She nodded yes. "Budget cuts."

Before you can say a blot of mustard, a crumb of cheese, we were walking through a cemetery. Prudence took me to a small group of people who were standing around a little hole. It was Ted and some of his friends. And there was a very fancy casket there, closed and ready to be buried. I was awful scared, but I tried to hide it. There was also a priest, and Ted looked really sad.

"Whoa," I said to Prudence, "Ted'll really go all out for me, won't he?"

"No, Mr. Fabio, this isn't your funeral. It's for Mr. Ted's new cat, Precious."

My mouth dropped open. "Precious? Who the hell is Precious?"

"Because of your severe behavior problems, Mr. Ted had to give you away to an elderly couple that lived outside of the city. He thought their farm might be just the place for you."

"But I'm just having fun with the big guy. He gets a stupid old girl cat and names her Precious?"

"That's not the way he looks at it. Mr. Ted couldn't keep you any longer. He was going to be evicted after you murdered the manager's iguana." Prudence said.

All of a sudden the two of us were at a farm out in the country where an old lady was milking a cow. Prudence had a nose clip 'cause the smell was so bad. I kind of cheered up, though, because there was lots of space to run around and lots of birds to chase—even though the place smelled a little skanky. "This isn't so bad," I said. "I think I'll enjoy this place."

Prudence pointed her umbrella over toward a small truck that was coming up the dirt road. I sensed it wasn't a friendly neighbor paying a visit. A real mean-looking guy got out of the truck, and the old woman handed him a small package.

"Mr. Fabio, you were never meant to be a country cat. If you were, you wouldn't have been run over by a tractor." And with that, Prudence showed me what was inside the package: It was me! It was me, and I was flatter than a pancake! And then she showed me what was inside the truck. There were other dead animals! Oh, my God! The guy with the truck was from a glue factory!

I'm glad Prudence was holding me, 'cause I passed out. When I woke up, I was looking into Ted's face. Then I saw my vet standing by Ted, and I heard him say I was going to make it. I was going to make it!

Ted thinks the electricity fried my personality. I think I was just going through a phase, and now I've grown up. I mean, God, I used to be so immature. What a dork! Besides, Ted really pampered me when we first got back from the vet's, and I just don't get the same pleasure

"I was awful scared but I tried to hide it."

that I used to in making his life a living hell. Meanwhile, he's finally met a nice girl, named Amy, and when the three of us are together, we're a pretty happy little family. They'll make a gourmet dinner and eat by candlelight, while I chew on the old *Well-Behaved Cat* tape. Amy's a little allergic to me, but whenever she sneezes, I sneeze with her. And then Ted exclaims aloud, "God bless us everyone!"

Lucky:
Who Turned Out the Light?

JOHNNY WAS FINED a hundred dollars by the Fish and Game authorities, and after I recovered the local SPCA took me away and put me in a new home. Look, I was ready to forgive and forget, but I guess all it takes is a cat to be shot by a hunter to really galvanize a community. Other hunters being shot is not so bad as the killing of an innocent housepet.

Well, I'm back on my lucky streak. Thankfully, my new owners turned out to be a real nice couple named Kevin and Jill, and they had two lovely children named Spencer and Phoebe. They sure took good care of me, because Kevin and Jill both hate guns and thought my little accident out in the woods was just awful. Why, I was so pampered and loved that at times it seemed like I was back in heaven with God and my guardian cats.

And there were lots of new things to discover. Once, after I tipped over the wastepaper basket, I found some old mint-flavored toothpicks. I was gnawing on them when Jill came in. She gently reprimanded me, and suddenly stopped cold. I saw her scrutinize a crumpled Visa bill. Then she tipped the basket over again, and she began tearing through the garbage with a vengeance. She became hysterical.

She went to the closet, pulled out a suitcase, and began packing. When Spencer and Phoebe came home from school, she sent them out to the car with the luggage. Kevin showed up and seemed very confused, until Jill showed him a bunch of receipts. She told Kevin he could take care of me because she and the children were going to a hotel. Then they were gone and I never saw them again.

I missed Jill and Spencer and Phoebe, but I particularly missed the furniture. See, some strange men had come and taken all the furniture and other stuff, so that all that was left was a bar stool and the refrigerator.

I felt sorry for Kevin, so I'd rub up against him and try to make him feel better. He started sneezing and getting really itchy eyes. He said this one rash he developed cost him an account. To try to stop his allergies, Kevin started taking this medicine. It must have been expensive, because he was always out of money and one of his relatives was treating him really badly, 'cause he kept saying how he wished Uncle Sam would get off his back. I guess Kevin couldn't pay our bills, because one night all the electricity went off. We were alone in the dark bare apartment, but Kevin said not to worry, that we were gonna be okay. He picked me up and petted me while he ordered a pizza and beer. Then he had to race to the medicine cabinet for his allergy medicine.

I can tell you now, that medicine does not mix with pizza. He started slurring his words, and after he finished the pizza, he lost his balance. He tripped over me and fell to the floor, landing on his face with a crack. He turned and looked at me with the strangest expression, and not only because he'd just broken his nose. The longer he stared, the more frightened I got. Kevin looked like he hated me with every fiber of his being. Finally he said that he understood now what was wrong and that he never should have gotten a black cat. He was trying to blame me for everything that happened, which is really absurd, isn't it? After all, I'm named Lucky.

But Kevin didn't see it that way. He took a broken bottle and started chasing me all over the house. And the language he was using! It would have shocked a pirate. I tried to reason with him, but he pretended he couldn't understand my meows. He sure could run fast for a drunk middle-aged man, but I guess that just shows how you can do anything if you put your mind to it.

At least I got a seventh chance to say hello to my heavenly guardians. Now that I think about it, they seemed kind of surprised to see me again, but I wasn't going to get too upset, by anything, because I figured I was earning frequent dying miles. Get it. Frequent dying miles. Ha ha ha.

Who am I kidding?

Freckles's Story:
And She's Cli-i-imbing a Sta-ir-way to Heaven

Hɪ! ᴍʏ ɴᴀᴍᴇ'ꜱ ꜰʀᴇᴄᴋʟᴇꜱ. It's almost my birthday. Right now I'm three months and a half. I'm not the runt of the litter. I can chase things and get them. I'm brave. I died once. There were angels and beautiful music and lots and lots of cat toys. They had drapes that you can climb up and nobody yells at you. And they have fields of flowers that you can smoosh, and no one gets really upset. And you can pee anywhere and nobody would say that you're gonna be an outside cat. Shh . . . Here comes someone. They can't see me here behind this plant. Wow, do you see that? There's something attacking their shoe. It's flopping around, holding on for dear life. I go in closer. Slowly. Quietly. Now I stop. Hold my breath. Crouch low. And pounce. Got it! No, wait. Whoa. I can kill the meanest of chewlaces. Sometimes I eat bugs. They don't taste very good, but they're fun to catch. Last week was when I almost died. It was 'cause I was attacked by Nitty Needles. He's one of those mean two-toothed yarny things that lives in a basket by the couch. He changes his shape really easily. He can go from being a ball to being really stringy to being like a sweater. He's like an octopus, 'cause he has big yarny testicles. They can grab hold of you and not let go. I wasn't doing anything. Just minding my own business. And I saw Nitty on the couch. I knew Mommy wouldn't like that so I tried to tell him to get off, but he wouldn't listen to me. I tapped him to get his attention. Not very hard. But he rolled away. And then, um, what he did was, he hit me. So then I hit him back. He tried to run away. I wouldn't let him off that easy. We struggled. It was a really big fight. I pulled out some of his hair. He was being naughty and I got kinda tangled up, but that was okay because at least he couldn't run away again. But then, somehow he started to strangle me. I wasn't scared really, but I thought of Mommy's and

Daddy's bed, and how sometimes I can hide under there and no one can find me. Maybe Nitty Needles wouldn't find me there. I pulled and pulled and pulled but it always stayed around my neck. Then I fell to the floor only I didn't hit the floor. I was just hanging there. Nitty was holding onto me and his mean old needly teeth were sticking up at me from the basket below. Then I couldn't breathe anymore. I couldn't meow. Everything went dark. That's when I flew. I don't think I was in my body, because I could see this little kitty that looked like me hanging from Nitty Needles, and I wasn't that little kitty anymore. I was just floating above old me. I liked flying. I was taller than anyone. Taller than older cats and taller than Mommy and Daddy. I meowed for Mommy and Daddy but they didn't hear me. I'm good at flying. I could fly to the top of trees and be higher than any other cats could ever climb. I wouldn't ever get stuck in trees, either. I could see everywhere. I could catch birds if I wanted and they wouldn't be able to escape because I could fly after them. When I died I heard this sound and then I looked over and there was this sort of tunnel. I thought it looked like a fun place to explore. And then I just flew right over there and I don't even know how it happened, 'cause I hadn't really practiced flying yet. That's why I know I was good at flying. And I started whizzing through this tunnel super fast. I could probably catch my tail, that's how fast I could go. And there was a light at the end of the tunnel, sort of like a headlight, but I know that I'm not supposed to go across the street in front of headlights or I'll get squished like my Aunt Tabitha. But I wasn't scared of the big light at all. Pretty soon it was all around me. The bright light felt warm and soft. Like rolling in clean towels out of the warm machine, before Mommy scolds me and puts me outside. Or like when I lick myself down below. Then I saw this stairway, so I raced up it. Then I raced back down. I like stairs. I raced up it again. And then at the top, I saw these big pearly doors. Underneath them I saw something go by, so I took a swat at it. I think I really scared it good, but then it came back. It looked sort of like a crumpled piece of paper, but I couldn't see it very well, even when I lay down and tried to peek underneath the door. So I just put my paws under the door and felt around for it. Whatever it was, it was pretty stupid because it kept coming back and letting me take swats at it. Then I heard someone on the other side of the door laugh. And then I caught my prey. I had it in both paws, but I couldn't pull it under the door. It was too big. It also wasn't struggling anymore. Boring. So I let go of it and was going to look around for something else to do. Then a man opened the door. He said his name was Peter. He asked me if I wanted

"I like stairs."

to come in. I sat down right where I was and licked
my paw. Then when he thought I wasn't interested I
darted in the door and found my prey. I pounced. Aha!
I got it! I had it in my mouth and was going to prance
out right back through the door. Then Peter picked me
up and said I was going the wrong way. He took my
prey from my mouth and said, "What do you want with
this old crumpled-up piece of paper?" Then he chuck-
led and set me down inside the gates. I got to roam all

around. You know what was neat about heaven? There were lots of cardboard boxes there that I could play in. They were really fun to roll around in. They also had sock drawers. Those are the best. God knows all the right places to scratch. And when I purred God called me a good girl. God knows Santa. God told me a joke. It's funny. You wanna hear it? Okay, How did the, I mean, Why did the cat walk on the beach? Because he wanted sandy claws. It's funny, huh? God said it's not my time yet. I don't know what that means. But after he said it I was back floating over the couch in our living room. Mommy and Daddy were there. The little kitty that I think was me, was out of Nitty Needles testicles and lying in Mommy's lap. Mommy looked so sad. She was crying. Why was Mommy crying? I thought about how I didn't want Mommy to cry. And then I wasn't floating anymore. It was dark and my neck hurt. I felt a tear fall on my face. I opened my eyes and saw Mommy. I tried to lift myself off her lap. Then I saw her smile. She cried and laughed at the same time. She gave me a big hug. That made me feel good. And I got better. And Nitty Needles was punished and sent to his basket. Now things are pretty much back to normal. Besides, Mr. Toilet Paper is a much better playmate than Nitty Needles ever was. And sometimes I still help Mommy and Daddy with those crumpled-up pieces of papers that like to hide behind doors. I don't know if they think those crumpled-up pieces of paper are alive or something because whenever they touch one, they throw it like it's gonna bite them. I always put on a good show of trying to kill it for them so they won't be scared. But I know it's already dead. I wasn't just born yesterday you know. I'm almost four months old.

Lucky:
Light at the End of the Tunnel

YES, FOLKS, I WAS PUT BACK TOGETHER in no time. Why, I didn't even make it through the entire tunnel after Kevin's attack. And it's amazing what vets can do these days. But I confess, if I hadn't met God firsthand, I'd have sworn he was playing some cruel practical joke on me.

Jill was so furious with Kevin she wanted to press charges. Instead, I heard he only gets to see Phoebe and Spencer on supervised visits. Jill and the kids moved to a nice old farm, and they spoiled me rotten. I got fresh milk for breakfast. They'd let me help in the garden where I kept the birds away from the strawberries. And ever since I brought them the special gift I found in the barn, they called me the champion mouser.

You'd think I would've been happy, but I was feeling pretty nervous. I mean, all cats have nine lives, right? Well, take it from me, after seven you start feeling a little bit skittish. And you know, when you're trying to be careful it only makes things worse. I'd been tense, jittery, and overwrought. Since the hunting accident I'd developed a fear of guns, backfiring cars, and popcorn. After my experiences with the dryer, garage door, and stove, I had a problem with most mechanical devices. I hid whenever an airplane flew by, and broken glass sent me scurrying for safety. You can see I was headed for disaster.

And unfortunately, it was disaster number eight. I was meandering through the meadow, keeping away from loud sounds, appliances, and bottles when I heard a noise. I admit I may have overreacted. At the time, I didn't know it was a bullfrog. I thought it might have been some newfangled twelve-gauge flying gas dryer with a mind of its own. So sue me! He was really close to me, and really loud, and I was startled. At any rate, I freaked and ran. Then it happened. I fell straight down into an old abandoned well. The good news was that there wasn't any stagnant old water. The bad news was, there wasn't any water.

Phoebe must've seen me run because she came after me. Right after me. I wish I could have warned her. At least I broke her fall.

On my way up to heaven, I reminded myself to have a little chat with God. I mean, eight is just too damn close to nine.

Leopold's Story:
Blinded by the Light

SHAKESPEARE ONCE SAID that death was "the undiscovered country from whose bourn no traveler returns." To this I retort, "nonsense." For I journeyed into the valley of the shadow of death, and I had a round-trip ticket. Before my romp in the Elysian Fields, I ridiculed anyone or anything. In fact, I delighted in making others miserable. I'd steal the last piece of jigsaw puzzles. Then I'd sit back and cheerfully watch the imbeciles search for a piece of cardboard sky thinking, For God's sakes, find a better use of your time! I'd break the heirloom

Limoges and make it look like the neighbor child did it. What bliss to watch his mother pull him home by his ear. I'd impregnate a female and leave her without looking back. Granted that runs in the species, but I was a first-class miscreant. I was hedonistic and selfish. I was not religious. I had no faith whatsoever, and I had never even entertained the possibility that our spirits might endure after our bodies did not. But since I have started talking about my ascension, I've met many other cats just like me who've gone through similar, albeit less fascinating experiences. And because my near-death experience was so vivid, realistic, and profound, I am now a totally changed feline.

A thunderstorm was rolling into D.C. on the night I died. From my perch on the answering machine I could see lightning bolts streak across the sky. Though I wouldn't have admitted it, I never liked lightning much, even from my early kittenhood. I must have sensed that lightning would always be my nemesis, that and the ball with the bell, but I digress.

Although I was nervous, I wouldn't budge an inch from where I was sitting quite comfortably erasing my owner's messages. When the phone rang and the machine picked up, I was so startled I nearly jumped out of my skin. Still, I stubbornly held my ground. Then it happened: Lightning struck the utility pole just outside our house, traveled through the phone wires, through the jacks, right into the answering machine, and in turn, into me. Electricity sizzled through my body. The thunderous roar deafened me. I couldn't even hear my own shrieking yowl. I was blinded by the light. I felt like a charcoal briquette, glowing red from the inside, and burned black on the outside.

The pain, though searing in its intensity, was brief. Soon I felt complete relief. I didn't know if I was in shock. I remember thinking it was miraculous that I was still cognizant. I wondered why I hadn't lost consciousness. I could see the room around me, the chaise longue, the coffee table, the Steinway. Everything looked normal, until I noticed that I was actually viewing the room from above. I was hovering near the ceiling. I had a passing fancy that maybe the lightning strike had given me the ability to fly. Then, as I floated over the machine, I saw that my charcoal-briquette analogy was fairly accurate. Seeing my own blackened body below me, I had an epiphany: I was dead.

As soon as I realized that I was no longer among the living, a tunnel formed. I heard a whirring noise and was sucked into the tunnel like a dead goldfish being flushed down a commode. At the center of the tunnel was a bright light, no bigger than a common field mouse. But it grew bigger and bigger as I approached.

It filled me with feelings of love that weren't at all claustrophobic, like when some cat fancier drops in unexpectedly at our house and is determined to pick me up. I had no urge whatsoever to claw the hell out of the light when it embraced me. Its unconditional love left me dumbfounded; I could hardly believe that no matter what I had done, I was loved. And as it hugged me tightly I began to see a movie of my life and what exactly I had done. It was not a enjoyable film. Even the Disney marketing department could not make anyone want to see this dud. I saw how disagreeable, offensive, and beastly I had really been. And from the opening images to the final lightning strike I felt all the pain my selfish ways had caused.

In my kittenhood I had over three thousand cat fights. In the movie of my life, I relived every single one of them, but now I was on the receiving end. I felt the emotions and sensations that my opponents had experienced. I felt the humiliation and mental torment of every one of my victims, even the ones who got just what they deserved.

I saw the pain I had caused my mother. I had relished the anguish I used to cause her and would brag to friends about how she couldn't control me and how much I hurt her. Now I felt that hurt, and it hurt. Oh, Mother, forgive Leopold his ills!

It wasn't my fault that I was hyperactive. I was undiagnosed and untreated. Back then they didn't have Ritalin. So I had to watch more of my misbehavior. I hissed and spat at anyone who was different. If I couldn't find cats from my own neighborhood, I prowled for others to beat up. I tortured baby birds instead of quickly putting them out of their misery.

Fortunately I wasn't rotten all the time. For instance, when a child was trying to pull a lizard's tail off, I jumped on the young ruffian and clawed at him until he freed the poor reptile. Unfortunately I wasn't always nice to other animals. I saw other occasions when I myself pulled tails off of the cold-blooded creatures. And I used to love to sit just out of range of the neighbor's chained dog, Spike, and watch as he barked and choked himself silly. The idiot!

As my film wound to a close I realized that hurting someone for fun hurts far worse than when you hurt someone for a good reason. When the film was over I was mortified at what a selfish, angry, vile cur I had been. If each mean act had been a single hair, I'd have had a furball the size of Gstaad. I thought for sure the Being of Light was going to curse my very existence. But to my relief, I felt only love and joy, as he forgave me and my guilt receded. The absolute kindness made such an impact on me. I learned the meaning of unconditional love, regardless of race, color, or breed.

The light started to move away, but I heard a parting message "Remember, cats are strong spirits who were sent to inspire others to be wondrous and whimsical." I see it so clearly now. I wish I had known it earlier.

My journey continued. I was brought to a heavenly valley where there was a shimmering city. Inside the city was a beautiful building, clear as if it had been made from Waterford. And inside the building were several spirit beings. They each glowed with light, which made the building look from the outside like an odd crystal pumpkin. Even from the inside I didn't know if I was in a courthouse, cathedral, or television studio. TV screens were everywhere. It was here that the beings revealed several messages to me.

The first screen showed loving people everywhere. They all spoke in a cloying baby talk to every cat they met. All over the world came the sounds of "Idn't dat a tweet kitty tat?" Horrifying.

The second was perhaps even more ominous. A world gone eco-crazy. Trash cans didn't exist. Only recycling bins.

The third showed a new electronic and digital world, a ghastly world without toys. No packing material, no paper clips, no desks covered with paper to mess.

"I was brought to a heavenly valley where there was a shimmering city."

The fourth television contained images of destruction. Cats were being neutered and spayed left and right. Frightening does not even begin to describe *les coupes des kitties*.

The fifth box showed happy children. This was perhaps the most scary vision of all. Children roamed villages looking to adopt pets. In particular, one terrifying image stayed with me; that of a tot racing up behind a cat on a diving board and startling him into the swimming pool.

The sixth revealed images of a once intelligent nation that stupidly kept putting dog owners in the White House. This was the only box that had a single positive aspect. It ended with a vision of a cat marking in the Lincoln Bedroom.

The final screen was a sort of summation of the others. With it came the message that the world I had just been shown would probably become a reality. Then came the bombshell: It was up to me to help cats learn how to live in this world. No longer would I think television was overrated.

I was told of my mission, which was to build several devices. The first was a refrigerator under which cat toys could not disappear. This, it was explained to me, would help cats retain some pleasure in their lives. I was also told to build a birdbath that repelled birds. The purpose of a birdless birdbath was unclear to me at first. Later I learned that as cats waited and waited and waited, they would learn much-needed patience. Finally, I was told to go out and create a human-size bed that was to be used for felines only. Everyone knows that human furniture, particularly a four-poster feather bed with high-thread-count linen, is much more comfortable than any cat furniture, and this large bed would provide soothing relief for tense cats. It would also let us get in touch with our calmer side with plenty of room for fabulous yawning, stretching, and kneading.

I had no idea how I was going to go about accomplishing this mission. First off, I had never built anything, and had no construction background. Second, I had no cash or English-speaking ability. Last, and most significant, I was dead.

The spirit beings read my thoughts, and, after admonishing me about being a wise-ass, they told me that I would find a way. Then they sent me back to earth.

My body had been taken to the nearest veterinary hospital. Apparently the caller, who was leaving a message when the lightning struck, somehow heard the explosion and my own screech, and he raced over immediately. Now, at the vet hospital, I hovered over myself in the operating room. I stared at my burned remains in disbelief. I felt reticent about going back into that still-smoking body, but I knew that I must in order to complete my mission. The next thing I experienced was excruciating pain.

Recovery was a long and arduous process. For many weeks I heard ringing in my ears. I was blind and paralyzed and could only just keep pondering ways that I might complete my mission. I was determined to build a refrigerator with a toy guard, a birdless birdbath and human-size cat bed. When I was finally up on my paws and coherent, friends told me it couldn't be done. When I rambled incessantly, fixated on my experience, my friends did not discourage me . . . for, alas, I had no friends. They would no longer return my catcalls. But I didn't give up. I couldn't.

Then a strange thing happened. I developed extrasensory perception, somehow as a result of the lightning strike. And I'm a much better cat since I stopped using my ESP to bet on the dogs. I have been able to save some money and I can actually say I'm making a difference in the lives of many cats. For now, you see, I'm not ashamed to tell my story. Furthermore, if it makes this book sell a million copies, my mission will be one step closer to becoming reality.

For I am not just any cat . . . I am Leopold! You see, I have changed.

Lucky:
Enough With the Light Already

Times Daily News

Circulation: 1,001,000   Sunday, 13th of May $1.00
Daily News Company, A Division of Tokyne Times Fun Corporation ®

Special Report
U.S. Holds Breath

By MOLLY WHITE

Across the country, people are glued to their television sets for coverage of the dramatic rescue of a cat and child from an old well. Thousands have flocked to the sleepy little town of Kimball which was unprepared for the media barrage that started yesterday afternoon. Marline Duncan found herself selling coffee to reporters from around the globe. Pocketing her small tip, she was overheard saying "I guess they don't pay Sam Powal from enough."

Meanwhile pjarch izel bekat jabcil thops zt.rim rashrca daefrgoh. Tiajek Lumon fpuod hqrest teulvg cwtae by repatbr scod aernfi teg hlibe. Qcjekilg mer nalpi ops tzabits ovqrdein xapnt bz uels aho mikt dix trm

Heroic kitty, Lucky, before she attempted to rescue child.

Peace In the Balkans

By LEN WOOLF
Associates Press

BELGRADE-The signing of today's treaty between Serbs and Croats, signifies the end of the war here. A28

Old Well Investigated

By LARRY AVERBACH

Yesterday's near disaster was all the more tragic because like so many falls down old wells, it could easily have been averted. A3

Cat Risks Life For Owner

By TIMOTHY CURTIS DIDLAKE

KIMBALL, MN- After 18 intense hours, the drama here is over. At approximately two o'clock yesterday afternoon, Lucky, the aptly named black cat of Till Durant and her family, survived a death-defying plunge into an old well while trying to save young Phoebe Durant. Thanks to Lucky, Phoebe survived, sustaining injuries only to her finger and her jaw. Lucky is listed in serious condition, but veterinarians expect a full recovery for the heroic feline.

Due to the nature of Phoebe's injuries the circumstances surrounding the accident are unclear. Phoebe is unable to talk because of her broken jaw, and cannot write with her broken fingers.

Ebcxun tich rbldem jno otai knpzo wukl nouz efbgro aglenk hzofef iks qrksa ibcnsa hujei klondz ina ovjan. Alvc przixmaln ztcoi desjiers na Hi Cubni, jcoka tlywa med wiato fjizl dunpoi tuxi faejy swhiv doei dno. If you're really trying to read these articles, get a life. Kojy Inkja'se izod hejt ifnt rvize, spst injuoe sply apze rfoge jera awlo mule nopl it sxeinju bacde ofe varjike snde xpot azi rnovk yfo tore islnsn jadu tnkzi atu kon. Lzane mixt spramt ekald idis ah txtreo grmit. Tash's zvaut kazbe awxo fike brte ajic anowu rizkl ablae.

Weather Threatens Tim
Didlake Day Parade C2

AFTER "BABY" PHOEBE CAME TO, she began to make noises. Though she sounded unintelligible with her broken jaw, she did attract attention. A lot of attention. We became a national news story. The media circus aired "Baby Phoebe Watch—Day One." We were rescued by the beginning of Day Two. Then the media tried to save face after finding out that Baby Phoebe was actually twelve years old. Suddenly I became the focus of the story. My picture was in all the papers, and with all the flashbulbs going off, I thought I'd nearly died once again. The media never heard the truth because Phoebe couldn't talk and she broke all her fingers.

You know, I find it just appalling that the media can probe into your past. They completely wrecked my life with Jill and Spencer and Baby Phoebe when word got out that Kevin had tried to kill me. And then someone remembered reading about the hunting accident. This led to the discovery of the attempted suicide and eventually to the plane wreck. The worst part is the rumors that have started and are being devoured as truth. Some economists claimed that I caused the recent stock market low. Both the Republicans and Democrats in Congress are blaming me for their gridlock. And a cowboy in San Antonio is blaming me for the Alamo. Meanwhile, Faye Dunaway has been pegged to play me in the musical based on my life, and now Jill thinks I really am bad luck. She quietly put me up for adoption. But don't cry for me. Remember, my name's Lucky! I may finally get the opportunity to complete the mission my guardian cats mentioned now that I've got a job. I've just been hired by the Acme Tennis Racquet and Violin Strings Company.